How to Generate Leads worth Hundred of millions: Making Strangers Want to Purchase Your Stuff

Douglas E. Weeks

Copyright message

TABLE OF CONTENTS

Introduction

The Mastery of Persuasion

It takes both art and science to stand out from the competition and persuade them to choose your product in a world where options abound and choices appear limitless. A marketer can become a persuasive force and turn a struggling business into a thriving one by developing the capacity to make customers crave your services rather than just want them. We're glad you're here and thank you for reading "How to Generate Leads worth Hundred of millions: Making Strangers Want to Purchase Your Stuff"

We'll go on a journey through these pages that probes the very core of human decision-making and exposes the tried-and-true tactics that can make your items truly appealing. This book is your road map to success whether you're an entrepreneur trying to break into a crowded industry, a salesperson trying to surpass your goals, or a marketing enthusiast trying to master the art of influence.

We'll examine the deep effects of audience comprehension and show how a solid foundation of familiarity with the target audience forms the basis for all persuasive arguments. You'll learn the value of problem-solving and how to position your items as the answers to problems encountered in everyday life. We'll mentor you in the craft of storytelling so you can establish emotional bonds with your audience and pique their interest in what you have to offer.

We'll talk about how developing credibility and trust is essential to the art of persuasion rather than a luxury. We'll demonstrate how to make the most of customer trust, explain your knowledge clearly, and use social proof to your advantage. And in an increasingly digital environment, we'll work with you to establish a compelling web presence so that your product captures consumers' attention right away.

However, how you say something is just as important to persuasion as what you say. We'll look at persuasive language and how to utilize words to elicit feeling, urgency, and action. The pages that follow will teach you how to address issues and objections, write persuading sales content, and guide customers toward making a purchase.

We'll explain the psychology behind discounts, freebies, and limited-time deals because incentives are effective instruments in the art of persuasion. You'll learn about powerful call-to-action tactics and conversion strategies that can convert inactive surfers into engaged customers.

Finally, we'll stress the value of client interactions and feedback. A devoted customer base and long-lasting success can be attained by developing close relationships with your customers, professionally addressing their questions and criticisms, and utilizing these insights to improve your goods and services.

This book is a practical handbook with applicable advice and examples drawn from real-world situations rather than merely a compilation of marketing theories and tactics. So let's start this adventure together. By the time you finish reading these pages, you'll be equipped with the skills necessary to master the art of persuasion and turn your goods into irresistible commodities.

Chapter 1

Understanding Your Audience

Understanding your audience is the first step in effective persuasion and marketing. Your persuasive methods will be based on a solid understanding of your target market. This chapter will cover creating client personas, conducting in-depth market research, and the crucial value of understanding your audience.

The Importance of Understanding Your Target Market

Take aim at a target while wearing a blindfold. It's a hopeless endeavor. Similar to this, trying to convince your audience without knowing who they are clearly is a fruitless exercise. The demographic most likely to be interested in and benefit from your products is known as your target market. It is crucial to fully understand them so that you can cater your messaging, goods, and services to their unique requirements.

Carrying out market research

Comprehensive market research is the first step in understanding your audience effectively. You must respond to important queries like:

- Who are your likely clients?
- What are their racial, ethnic, and socioeconomic characteristics?
- What are their values, hobbies, and lifestyles (psychographics)?
What issues or requirements do they have that your product can help with?

Surveys, focus groups, interviews, and data analysis can all be used in market research. It's a combination of qualitative and quantitative methodologies that offer you insights into your audience's preferences, actions, and difficulties.

Establishing customer personas

The development of consumer personas is one of the most effective strategies for audience comprehension. A customer persona is a thorough, loosely fictional portrayal of your ideal client. It aids in giving your target market a name, a face, and a backstory. A persona usually consists of:

- Name and contact information
- Challenges and objectives
- Obstacles and pain points
- Favored channels for communication

You may effectively imagine your audience and make marketing decisions with them in mind by constructing personas.

If one of your personas is "Sarah, a busy working mom of two," for instance, you may modify your messaging and marketing tactics to appeal to her unique requirements and way of life.

Understanding your audience is a continuous process that develops along with your business and the shifting nature of the industry. You will have the fundamental information and resources at the end of this chapter to begin developing a thorough grasp of your target market, laying the groundwork for the persuasive strategies we'll examine in the subsequent chapters.

Chapter 2

The Ability to Solve Problems

Now that you've taken the first step toward understanding your audience, it's time to put this knowledge to use and become a master of persuasion. One of the most effective methods to attract consumers to buy your products is to position them as solutions to real-world problems. In this chapter, we'll look at the concept of problem-solving and how it may help your product stand out.

Identifying Needs and Problems

Every day, people face obstacles, inconveniences, and unmet needs. As a business owner or marketer, your goal is to identify these demands and pain points in your target market.

These might range from little annoyances such as tangled headphone wires to more important concerns such as managing personal money. If you are aware of the issues that your potential customers experience, you will be able to deliver more effective responses.

Positioning Your Product as a Solution

Once you've identified your audience's challenges and needs, the next step is to promote your product as a solution. This procedure consists of two steps:

1. Emphasizing the Advantages Explain in detail how your solution addresses their specific difficulties or requests. What are the primary advantages of your product over competitors? How does it improve, ease, or enhance your clients' quality of life? Pay attention to the outcomes of your product.

2. Creating Powerful Value Propositions: A value proposition is a concise explanation of

what potential purchasers would gain by using your product. It must stand out, be enticing, and be obvious. Your value proposition should answer the question, Your value proposition should address the following question: "Why should I choose your product over others?" This is your chance to recognize your items and show their value.

Desire Psychology

It is just as crucial to create desire for your products as it is to solve problems in order to convince people to buy them. The psychology of want is a complicated web of feelings, needs, and desires. Using this psychology, you can create an irresistible attraction for your items. Here's how:

- **Emotional Needs Compensation**: Recognize your audience's emotional requirements. Is it comfort, status, safety, or adventure that people seek? Make sure your product's messaging appeals to these emotional triggers.

-**Improving Urgency**: You can create a sense of urgency by leveraging the fear of missing out (FOMO) or the expectation of future benefits. Limited-time specials, one-of-a-kind promos, and seasonal exclusivity are all common methods.

-**How to Use Social Proof**: Individuals are more likely to want what others have. Provide success stories, client testimonials, and case studies to illustrate that your product is desired and trusted by others.

-**Picking up on Aspirations**: Your product can divide where your clients are and where they want to be. Describe how your product will assist them in achieving their ambitions or goals by appealing to their aspirations.

It is strong in the art of persuasion to be able to portray your product as a solution to real-world problems while also evoking desire. By the end of this chapter, you'll be able to establish marketing messages and methods that will boost the appeal of your products and persuade potential consumers that your products are exactly what they're looking for.

Chapter 3

Creating Convincing Narrative

Stories have an exceptional capacity to interface with people on a profound, individual level. They summon feelings, make ideas engaging, and can be a powerful device in influence. In this part, we'll dive into the specialty of narrating and how it can change your items into enamoring and extraordinary contributions.

The Craft of Narrating in Marketing

Narrating is a characteristic piece of the human experience. We learn, understand, recollect through stories. In promoting, it's the tales you tell about your items and your image that have an enduring effect. Successful narrating can:

- Produce a remarkable association with your crowd.
- Make your message more critical.
- Pass on complex thoughts and data in a connecting with way.
- Bring out feelings that drive activities.

Creating a Brand Narrative

Your image is something other than a logo or a name; it's the story you describe about your organization. A brand story characterizes the pith of your business, including its qualities, mission, and vision. It ought to respond to questions, for example,

- For what reason does your business exist?
- What values guide your choices?
- What excursion prompted your item or administration?
- How would you try to affect your clients' lives?

Your image story separates you from contenders and structures a novel association with your crowd. It assists clients with connecting with your image on an individual level.

Making Real Profound Associations with Your Audience

Feelings are strong inspirations. At the point when individuals feel genuinely associated with an item or brand, they are more disposed to want it. You can utilize narrating to inspire feelings that drive your crowd to make a move, including feelings like:

-**Empathy**: Offer stories that exhibit how you might interpret your clients' difficulties and trouble spots, causing them to feel appreciated and comprehended.

-**Joy**: Praise the examples of overcoming adversity and positive encounters your item has given to clients.

-Hope: Describe stories that motivate and represent a way to a superior future with your item.

-Adventure: Utilize stories that cause your crowd to feel like they're important for an interesting excursion, and your item is the way into that experience.

- Relatability: Offer stories that depict genuine individuals, very much like your clients, profiting from your item.

Placing It into Action

In this segment, you'll likewise figure out how to apply narrating to different parts of your showcasing procedure, including:

-Site and landing pages: Making connecting with and narrating centered web content.
- Social media: Creating posts and missions that recount a story and interface with your crowd

-**Advertising**: Planning promotions that inspire feelings and drive activity.

- **Email marketing**: Creating messages that vibe individuals and locking in.

Toward the finish of this segment, you'll have a more profound appreciation for the force of narrating and the devices to make convincing stories that not just make individuals need to buy your items yet additionally become sincerely put resources into them. Narrating is your unmistakable benefit to change your contributions from simple things on a rack into stories that profoundly resound with your crowd.

Chapter 4

Building Trust and Credibility

The basis of persuasion is trust. Your efforts to persuade customers to buy your products won't be successful without it. In this chapter, we'll look at how crucial it is to establish credibility and trust within your company and how doing so can improve the value of your products and services.

How Important Trust Is in Business

Any effective business connection is built on trust. It is the conviction that your business or brand will keep its commitments and produce benefits. Customers are more inclined to select your offerings, use your services, and show sustained loyalty when they have faith in you.

Trust-Building Strategies

1. Transparency Building trust requires being frank and up front about your goods, services, and company practices. Explicitly state what your items' capabilities are. Pricing for sharing, terms, and other pertinent policies are all disclosed.

2. Consistency: Consistency in your branding, customer experience, and messaging fosters a sense of dependability. Customers are more inclined to trust your brand if they know what to anticipate from it.

3. Dependability Delivering on your commitments on a regular basis is essential. This entails keeping deadlines, delivering top-notch customer support, and guaranteeing the quality of the final output. Trust arises organically when expectations are routinely met or exceeded.

4. Reviews and Testimonials from Customers Showcase positive customer experiences to use social evidence. Share client success stories from real people who have used your products or services via case studies, reviews, and testimonials.

5. Authority and Expertise: Promote your brand or yourself as a subject-matter authority. Through blogs, webinars, and workshops, you may impart your knowledge. People are more likely to trust your items if they perceive you as an authority.

6. Ethical business practices: Trust is fostered by ethical actions. Make sure your company upholds ethical standards in all of its transactions, from obtaining resources to marketing to dealing with clients.

7. Accessibility and customer support Trust may be greatly increased by offering top-notch customer service and being accessible to address queries and issues. Answer questions as soon as

possible and offer enlightening, beneficial guidance.

Leveraging Testimonials and Social Proof

Social proof is an intense instrument for laying out believability and trust. It is the idea that people frequently imitate others' behavior. Social proof can be used by:

- Prominently promoting positive client feedback and ratings on your website.
- Highlighting endorsements or alliances with reputable companies or influential people.
- Using numbers and statistics to show how well-liked or successful your items are.

The Prolonged Advantages of Trust

Trust is a long-term investment rather than merely a short-term aim. A customer who has faith in your brand is more likely to buy from you frequently and recommend your goods to others. Word-of-mouth advertising benefits from trust as well because happy consumers are more likely to do so.

You will comprehend the vital significance that credibility and trust play in convincing customers to choose your items at the end of this chapter. Your offerings will be more alluring and persuasive as a result of the tactics and resources you have to develop trust with your audience.

Chapter 5

Making an Interesting Online Presence

In the modern digital era, potential buyers frequently form their initial image of your company online. A company's ability to capture a customer's interest or risk losing them to the competition depends on how engaging their online experience is. We'll examine the essential components of developing an online presence that enthralls and persuades your audience in this chapter.

What's Important About Your Online Presence?

Your brand's overall online presence is represented by your online presence. It includes all of your audience's digital touchpoints, including your website, social media accounts, email correspondence, and others. Your online presence can have a big impact on your business in a world when online interactions, research, and purchase are the standard.

Creating websites that are user-friendly

The focal point of your online presence is frequently your website. A successful website should:

1. **Be visually appealing**: To create a good first impression, use clear, expert design and high-quality images.

2. **Load quickly**: Websites that take too long to load may lose visitors. Improve the performance of your website to keep users interested.

3. **Adapt to mobile devices**: Make sure your website is responsive and works effectively on smartphones and tablets given the increase in mobile browsing.

4. **Have a clear navigation**: Make it simple for visitors to locate the information they require by

providing them with user-friendly navigation menus.

5. **Provide valuable content**: Provide interesting, educational information that speaks to the wants and interests of your audience.

Making Use of Social Media Sufficiently

Platforms on social media are essential for creating and sustaining your online presence. Effective social media use involves

1. Select the appropriate platforms: Concentrate on the social media channels that are relevant to your target market. Every platform has its own distinct user habits and demographics.

2. Maintaining a regular posting schedule will keep your audience interested and informed.

3. Engage in discussion with your audience and reply to their comments and messages. A two-way correspondence road is virtual entertainment.

4. Share interesting stuff. To keep your content interesting and appealing, mix text with photographs, videos, and other media.

SEO and content marketing

The foundation of your internet presence is content. In order to draw in and keep the attention of your audience, content marketing entails developing and publishing worthwhile, pertinent material. Blog posts, articles, videos,

infographics, and other types of information can be included. Search engine optimization (SEO) is also essential to help your content rank higher in search engine results, increasing the likelihood that your target audience will find it.

Clear and persuasive copywriting

It matters what you write in your online persona. Writing compelling copy can:
- Express the unique benefits of your labor and products
- Create a feeling of excitement or urgency.
- Address typical defenses and reservations.
- Encourage site visitors to take action, such as buying something or subscribing to your newsletter.

Engaging in Online Marketing

Your internet visibility can be improved with the help of online advertising. Pay-per-click (PPC) ads, display ads, social media ads, and more options are available. The correct audience must be targeted, attractive ad material must be created, and campaigns must be optimized for maximum impact.

You'll have a strong understanding of the crucial components of building a compelling online presence by the end of this chapter. You'll be given the skills and methods you need to leave a lasting digital impression on your target market and ultimately persuade them that your items are worth their time and consideration.

Chapter 6

The Language of Persuasion

Words hold enormous power. They can illuminate, move, and, above all, convince. In this section, we'll investigate the complexities of language in advertising and how you can utilize the right words and expressions to make your items significantly really alluring.

The Impact of Words in Marketing

The words you pick can have a tremendous effect in your capacity to convince your crowd. Language can bring out feelings, make earnestness, and address complaints. This is the way you can outfit the impact of words:

-**Bringing out Emotion**: Close to home allure is a powerful influence. Words like "love," "trust," "happiness," and "motivation" can take advantage of profound sentiments and reverberate with your crowd. Utilize profound language that lines up with the feelings you believe your crowd should connect with your item.

-**Make Urgency**: Desperation is a typical strategy in showcasing. Phrases like "restricted time offer," "act now," and "while provisions last" can make a need to get moving, provoking possible clients to make a quick move.

-**Address Objections**: Your crowd might have reservations or protests about your item. Powerful copywriting tends to these worries. For instance, on the off chance that cost is a typical complaint, you can utilize phrases like "reasonable valuing" or "financial plan well disposed."

- **Feature Uniqueness**: Each item has something that separates it. Use words and expressions to grandstand what makes your item extraordinary. Whether it's "exceptional," "elite," or "unequaled," featuring uniqueness can make your item more attractive.

- **Stress Benefits**: Your clients are more intrigued by how your item can help them than its highlights. Use words to underscore the advantages of your item. For example, "efficient," "easy," and "groundbreaking" convey esteem.

Beating Protests and Concerns

It's fundamental to comprehend the protests and concerns potential clients could have about your item. Address these complaints head-on in your advertising materials. For example, on the off chance that one normal concern is solidness, you can incorporate expressions like "dependable" or "surefire quality."

Creating Convincing Deals Copy

Viable deals duplicate is an expertise that joins every one of the components examined in this section. This is the way to make convincing duplicate:

- Begin with areas of strength that snatch consideration and provoke curiosity.
- Use subheadings and list items to make the substance readable.
- Incorporate tributes, audits, and contextual investigations for social evidence.
- Be clear and compact, staying away from language or excessively specialized language.
- Make a feeling of stream and guide the peruser toward a source of inspiration (CTA).

Utilizing Enticing Language Across Advertising Materials

The language of influence ought to pervade your promoting materials, from your site to email missions to publicizing. Consistency in informing and language builds up your offer and has a more grounded effect.

A/B Testing and Language Optimization

In the computerized age, you can test the viability of your language through A/B testing. Explore different avenues regarding various titles, invitations to take action, and convincing language to recognize what reverberates most with your crowd.

Toward the finish of this section, you'll have an extensive comprehension of how language can be your most powerful device in influence. You'll be prepared to make convincing, influential promoting content that imparts the exceptional worth of your items and drives your crowd to make a move.

Chapter 7

Impetuses and Change Strategies

In the realm of influence and showcasing, impetuses assume an essential part in pushing expected clients to make a move. Whether it's making a buy, pursuing a pamphlet, or drawing in with your image somehow or another, offering impetuses and utilizing successful transformation methodologies can make your items seriously engaging and empower the ideal activities.

Figuring out the Brain research of Incentives

Impetuses tap into the brain science of human direction. They influence our regular tendency to look for remunerations and advantages. By offering impetuses, you can impact your crowd's way of behaving and increment their inspiration to draw in with your items or administrations.

Sorts of Incentives

1. **Discounts**: Giving a marked down cost or limited time special is perhaps the most well-known and compelling motivator. For example, offering a restricted time markdown or a rate off the standard cost can make a need to get moving and make your items more appealing.

2. **Freebies**: Giving something free of charge, whether it's a free item, an example, or a select download, can provoke curiosity and energize collaboration. Gifts can be especially viable in return for contact data or as a component of a buy.

3. **Loyalty Programs:** Laying out a faithfulness program rewards rehash clients with restrictive advantages, limits, or unique access. Such projects support client maintenance as well as construct brand steadfastness.

4. **Guarantees**: Giving an unconditional promise or a fulfillment diminishes the apparent gamble of making a buy. It exhibits trust in your item and consoles likely clients.

5. **Limited-Time Offers**: Time-delicate motivations, for example, streak deals or prompt riser estimating, make a need to keep moving and support quick activity. They influence the apprehension about passing up a great opportunity (FOMO).

6. **Contests and Giveaways**: Facilitating challenges or giveaways via virtual entertainment or your site can increment commitment and create fervor around your items. Members are attracted by the opportunity to win an award or acknowledgment.

Powerful Source of inspiration Strategies

A solid source of inspiration (CTA) is fundamental for directing your crowd toward the ideal activity. Consider these techniques to streamline your CTAs:

-Clear and Significant Language: Utilize immediate and clear language that rules out uncertainty. Phrases like "Purchase Presently," "Join Today," or "Get everything rolling" are direct and convincing.

- Make a Feeling of Urgency: Impart a feeling of promptness in your CTAs by adding phrases like "Restricted Time Proposition" or "Act Now." This drives your crowd to rapidly make a move.

- Utilize Visual Cues: Utilize plan components, like bolts or fastens, to cause you to notice your CTA. Make it outwardly unmistakable from the remainder of your substance.

-Feature Benefits: Obviously express the advantages your crowd will get by making the ideal move. For instance, "Save 20% Today" or "Open Particular Substance."

-A/B Testing:Investigation with various CTAs to figure out which ones are the best. A/B testing permits you to refine your methodologies in view of genuine crowd reactions.

Estimating the Effect of Motivators and Change Strategies

To measure the viability of your motivating forces and change procedures, you can utilize different measurements, for example, transformation rates, navigate rates, and return for money invested. Consistently dissect and change your procedures in light of the information you gather, guaranteeing you're persistently working on your methodology.

Toward the finish of this section, you'll have an exhaustive comprehension of the job motivators and change techniques play in making your items really engaging and empowering activity. You'll be furnished with the information and instruments to execute and quantify these techniques successfully, at last driving transformations and expanding the allure of your items.

Chapter 8

Client Connections and Feedback

A flourishing business doesn't exclusively depend on gaining new clients; it likewise relies upon supporting existing connections. In this section, we'll investigate the significance of building and keeping up major areas of strength with connections and how criticism can be an important device for item improvement and consumer loyalty.

Fabricating and Keeping up with Client Relationships

Building solid client connections is fundamental for long haul achievement. This is the way you can encourage and keep up with these associations:

1. **Personalized Communication**: Address your clients by name, propose custom-made suggestions, and show veritable interest in their requirements. Personalization causes clients to feel esteemed.

2. **Consistent Engagement**: Keep up with standard correspondence with your clients. Whether through email bulletins, online entertainment updates, or exceptional offers, remaining drew in keeps your image top of psyche.

3. **Exceptional Client Service**: Give responsive and accommodating client assistance. Fast reactions to requests and proficient issue goals show your obligation to consumer loyalty.

4. **Exclusive Offers and Reliability Programs**: Prize steadfast clients with elite offers, limits, or early admittance to new items. Dependability projects can boost rehash business.

5. **Feedback Collection**: Effectively look for and energize criticism from your clients. Show that their viewpoints matter, and be available to their ideas and reactions.

6. **Surprise and Delight**: Sometimes shock your clients with startling advantages or badges of appreciation. These little motions can go quite far in fortifying connections.

7. **Community Building**: Make a feeling of the local area around your image, where clients can communicate, share their encounters, and proposition backing to each other.

Taking care of Client Requests and Feedback

Successful treatment of client requests and input is critical for relationship-building. This is the method for getting it going:

1. **Prompt Responses**: Answer requests and criticism as fast as could be expected. Regardless of whether you can't give a quick

arrangement, recognizing their feedback or concerns is fundamental.

2. **Active Listening**: Effectively pay attention to your clients and look to figure out their points of view. This sympathy can stop tough spots and upgrade connections.

3. **Problem Resolution**: Work constantly to determine any issues or concerns raised by clients. A fruitful goal can transform a disappointed client into a reliable backer.

4. **Constructive Feedback**: Urge clients to give productive criticism. Their bits of knowledge can distinguish regions for development in your items and administrations.

Involving Criticism for Item Improvement

Criticism isn't only for settling quick issues; it's an important wellspring of experiences for working on your items. This is the way you can utilize client criticism successfully:

1. **Collecting Feedback**: Make channels for clients to give input, for example, reviews, idea boxes, and direct correspondence.

2. **Categorizing Feedback**: Arrange criticism into various sorts, for example, item related, client assistance, and client experience. This aids in focusing on upgrades.

3. **Analyzing Data**: Break down criticism information to recognize repeating examples and issues. Search for both positive and negative input.

4. **Implementing Changes**: In light of the experiences acquired from client criticism, roll out fundamental improvements and upgrades to your items and administrations.

5. **Communication**: Keep your clients informed about changes made because of their input. This builds up the possibility that their feedback matters.

The Advantages Areas of strength for of Relationships

Solid client connections offer various advantages:

- **Client Dedication**: Faithful clients are bound to rehash buys and prescribe your items to other people.

- **Expanded Deals**: Fulfilled clients are bound to investigate and buy extra items or redesigns.

- **Brand Support**: Blissful clients can become vocal backers, advancing your items through informal exchange and online audits.

- **Market Bits of knowledge**: Client input gives significant experiences to item improvement and promoting procedures.

- **Upper hand**: serious areas of strength for building can separate you from rivals according to your clients.

Toward the finish of this part, you'll comprehend the significant job areas of strength for that connections and criticism play in making your items really engaging and your business more effective. You'll be furnished with the information and procedures to assemble and keep up with these connections, eventually expanding the allure of your items and the development of your business.

Conclusion

Improving Your Business Persuasion Skills

The key to success in the competitive corporate environment is the capacity for persuasion. We've examined a multifaceted strategy that includes understanding your audience, problem-solving, storytelling, trust-building, online presence, persuasive language, incentives, and customer relationships as we've delved into the nuances of persuading people to buy your products throughout this book.

You now have the skills and knowledge necessary to not only design items that satisfy the needs of your customers but also to showcase those things in a way that inspires genuine desire in them. The concepts of persuasion are applicable and significant regardless of your level of experience as an entrepreneur or where you are in your company journey.

Keep in mind that the art of persuasion is about building trust and providing value, not about manipulating people. It involves developing services and experiences that connect with your target market, take care of their needs, and realize their dreams.

Keep in mind the dynamic nature of your audience, your market, and the digital environment as you use these concepts in your company. Keep an open mind, be receptive to criticism, and be prepared to change your tactics to best serve your clients. It takes time and persistent effort to develop enduring, meaningful relationships with your audience.

It takes time and effort to convince people to buy your items. Maintain your learning, experimentation, and approach-refinement. You may make people want to buy your products by continually working to understand your audience, communicate clearly, and offer outstanding value. You can also establish yourself as a reliable and powerful force in your business by consistently aiming to understand your audience.

Your quest to master the art of persuasion is far from over because the world of business is always evolving. As you work to fulfill the demands of your audience, keep learning, improving, and expanding. In doing so, you can create a company that actually resonates with customers and succeeds in a competitive market.